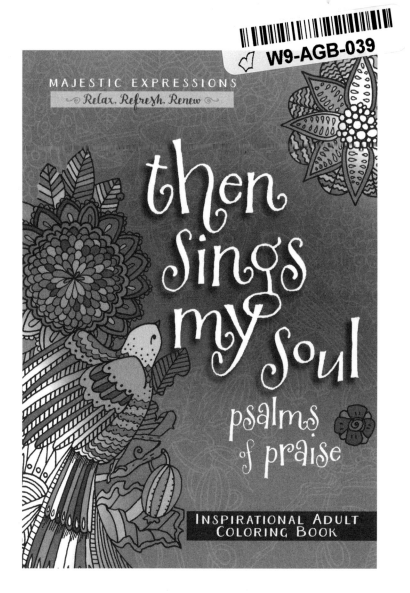

MAJESTIC EXPRESSIONS
Relax, Refresh, Renew

then sings my soul

psalms
of praise

INSPIRATIONAL ADULT
COLORING BOOK

BroadStreet
PUBLISHING

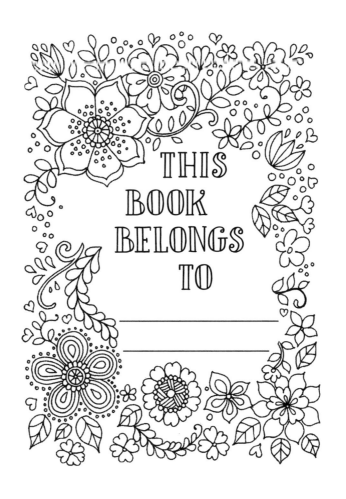

THIS
BOOK
BELONGS
TO

_____
_____

BroadStreet Publishing Group LLC
Racine, Wisconsin, USA
Broadstreetpublishing.com

MAJESTIC EXPRESSIONS

THEN SINGS MY SOUL: PSALMS OF PRAISE

© 2016 by BroadStreet Publishing

ISBN 978-1-4245-4976-4

Cover design by Chris Garborg | garborgdesign.com
Compiled and edited by Michelle Winger | literallyprecise.com

Printed in the United States of America.

16 17 18 19 20 21 22   7 6 5 4 3 2 1

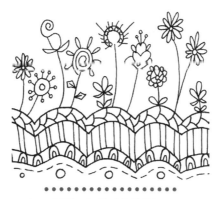

INTRODUCTION

There is plenty of research that shows coloring to be an effective stress reducer. Maybe you picked up this book because you've heard the hype and you're curious. Perhaps you've been looking for a way to relax. Now you have your very own adult coloring book, and you have every reason you need to sit down and color. And perforated pages make it easy for you to frame your favorites!

Coloring is a great distraction from all you have going on, but the best way to find lasting peace is to spend time with your Creator. Fill these intricately designed illustrations with the beauty of color as you dwell on the richness of his Word, the faithfulness of his character, and the depth of his love for you.

Happy coloring!

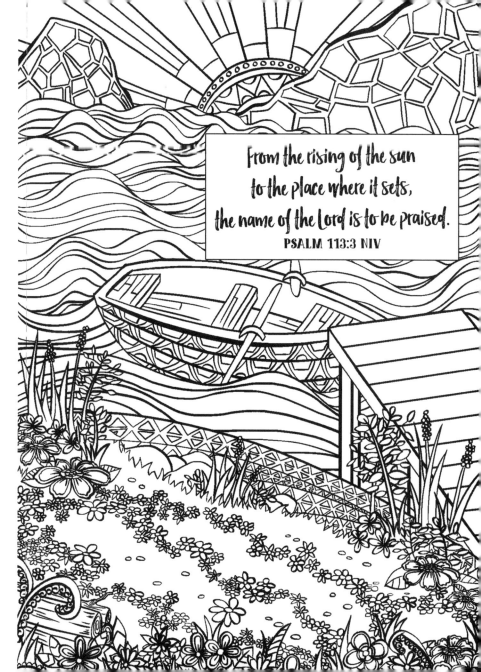

From the rising of the sun
to the place where it sets,
the name of the Lord is to be praised.

PSALM 113:3 NIV

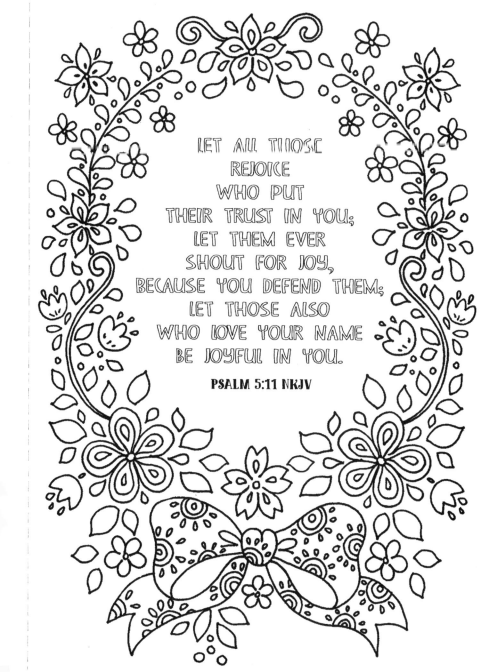

LET ALL THOSE
REJOICE
WHO PUT
THEIR TRUST IN YOU;
LET THEM EVER
SHOUT FOR JOY,
BECAUSE YOU DEFEND THEM;
LET THOSE ALSO
WHO LOVE YOUR NAME
BE JOYFUL IN YOU.

PSALM 5:11 NKJV

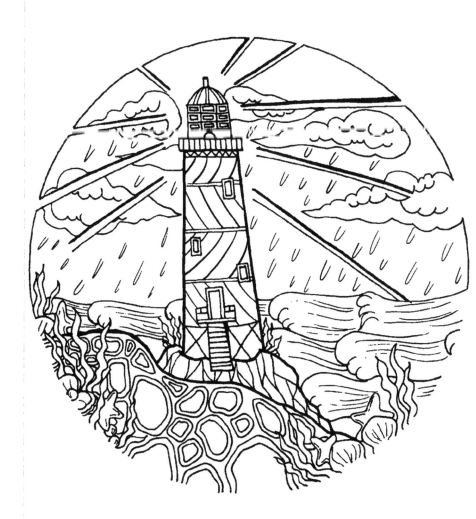

I will sing of your strength,
in the morning I will sing of your love;
for you are my fortress, my refuge in times of trouble.

PSALM 59:16 NIV

Praise the Lord. Sing to the Lord a new song,
his praise in the assembly of his faithful people.

PSALM 149:1 NIV

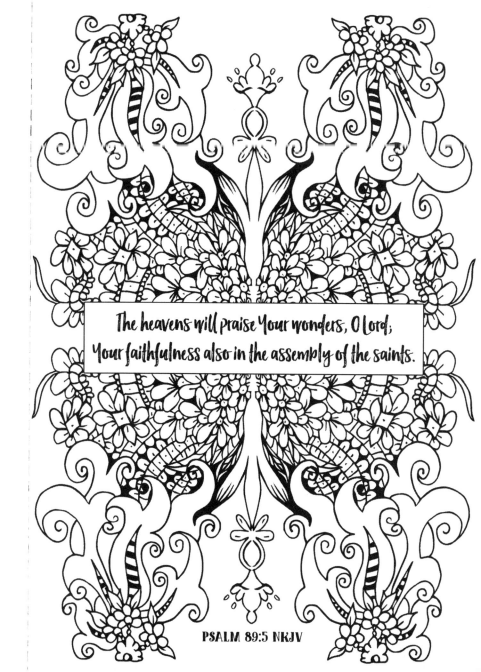

The heavens will praise Your wonders, O Lord;
Your faithfulness also in the assembly of the saints.

PSALM 89:5 NKJV

YOUR STEADFAST LOVE IS AS HIGH AS THE HEAVENS;

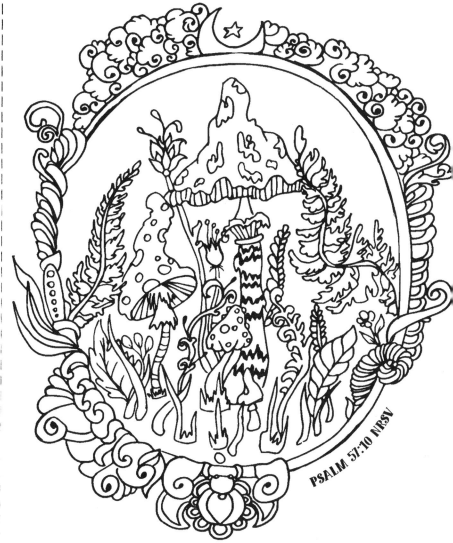

PSALM 57:10 NRSV

YOUR FAITHFULNESS EXTENDS TO THE CLOUDS.

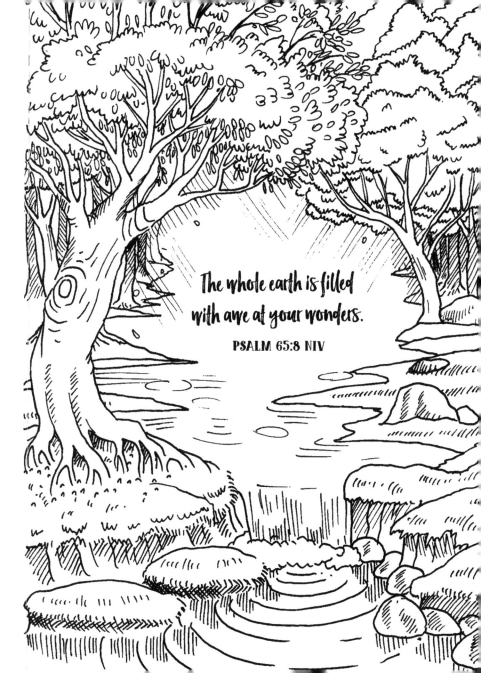

The whole earth is filled
with awe at your wonders.

PSALM 65:8 NIV

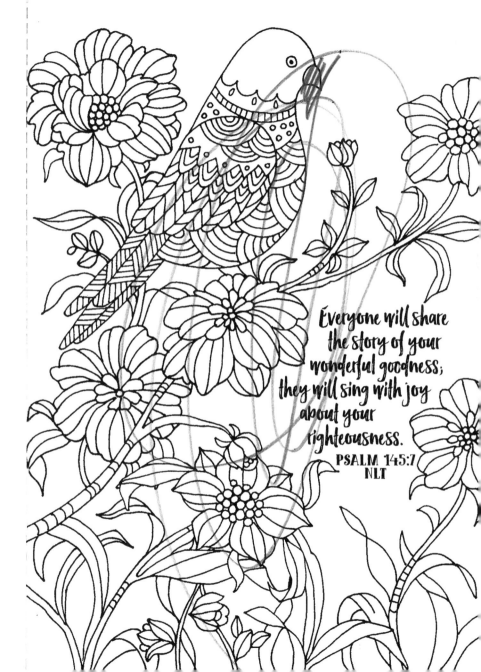

Everyone will share
the story of your
wonderful goodness;
they will sing with joy
about your
righteousness.

PSALM 145:7
NLT

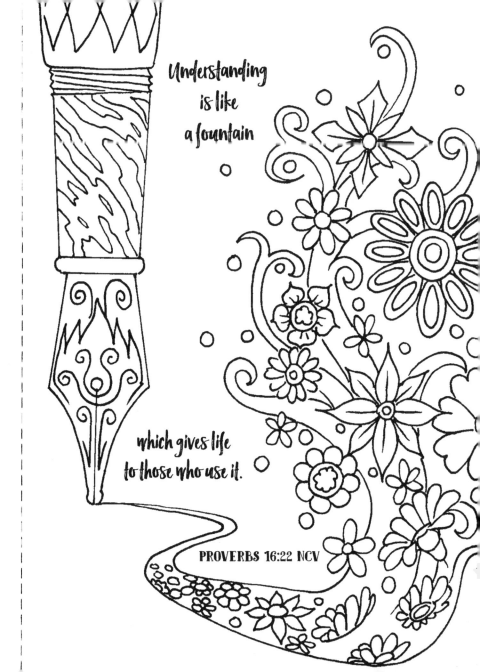

Understanding
is like
a fountain

which gives life
to those who use it.

PROVERBS 16:22 NCV

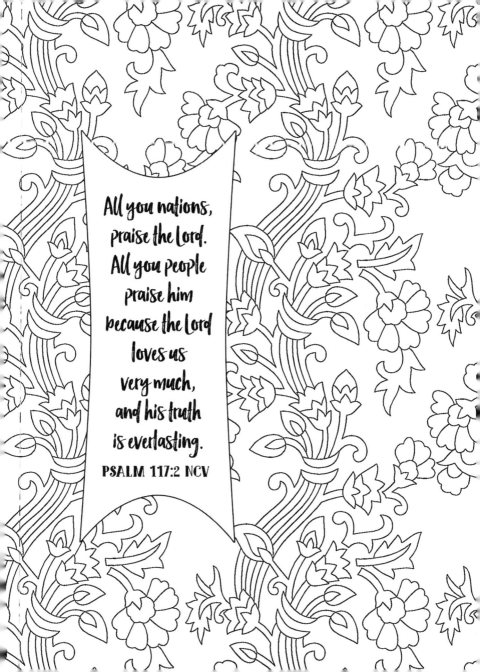

All you nations,
praise the Lord.
All you people
praise him
because the Lord
loves us
very much,
and his truth
is everlasting.

PSALM 117:2 NCV

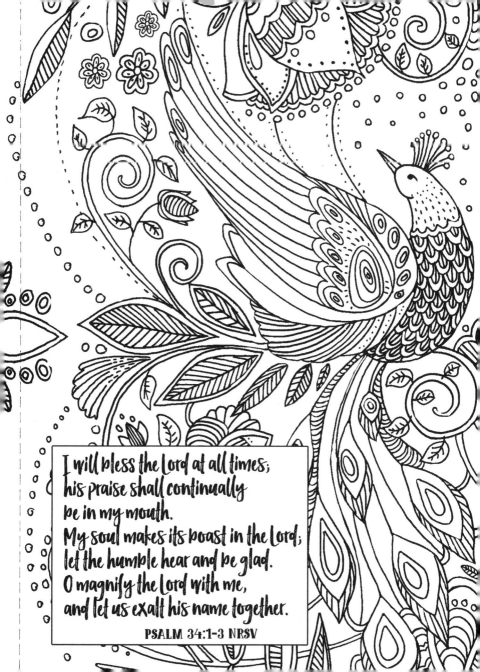

I will bless the Lord at all times;
his praise shall continually
be in my mouth.
My soul makes its boast in the Lord;
let the humble hear and be glad.
O magnify the Lord with me,
and let us exalt his name together.

PSALM 34:1-3 NRSV

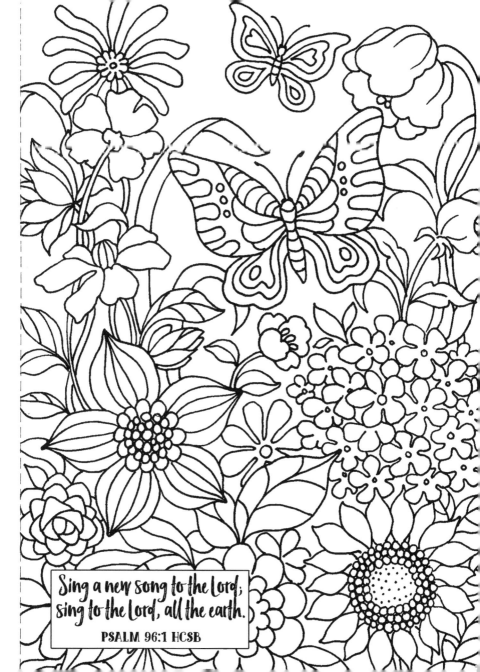

Sing a new song to the Lord;
sing to the Lord, all the earth.

PSALM 96:1 HCSB

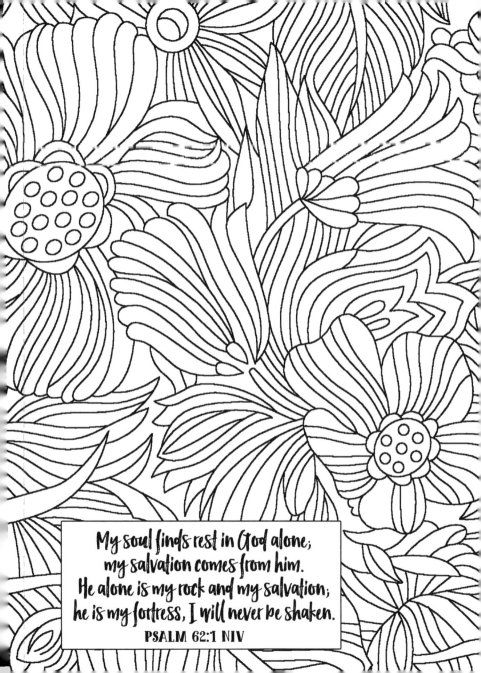

My soul finds rest in God alone;
my salvation comes from him.
He alone is my rock and my salvation;
he is my fortress, I will never be shaken.

PSALM 62:1 NIV

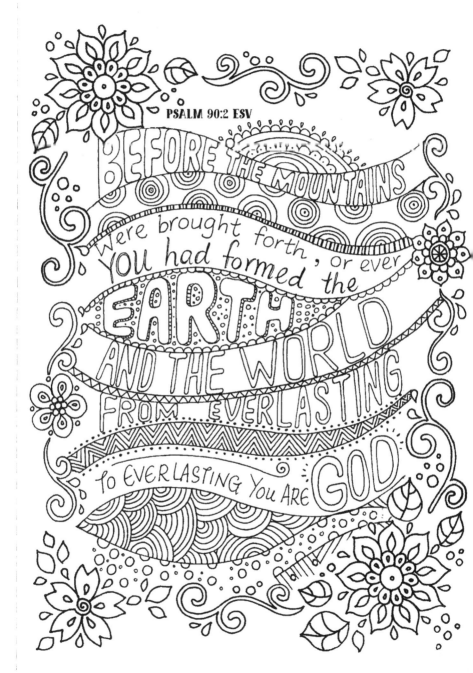

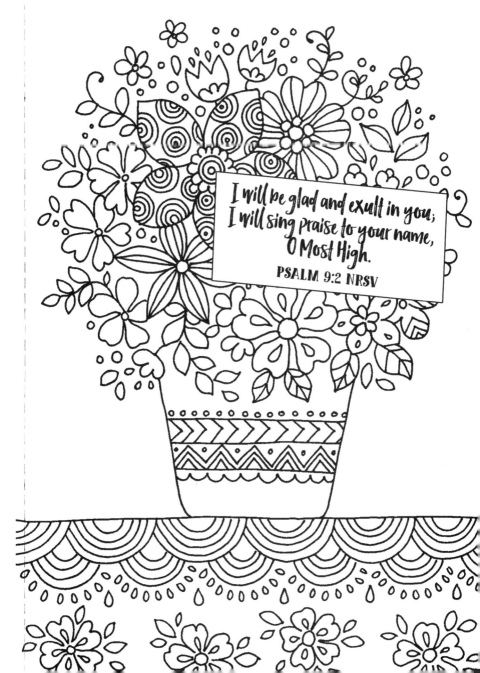

I will be glad and exult in you;
I will sing praise to your name,
O Most High.

PSALM 9:2 NRSV

You, O Lord, are a God of compassion and mercy,
slow to get angry and filled with unfailing love
and faithfulness.

PSALM 86:15 NLT

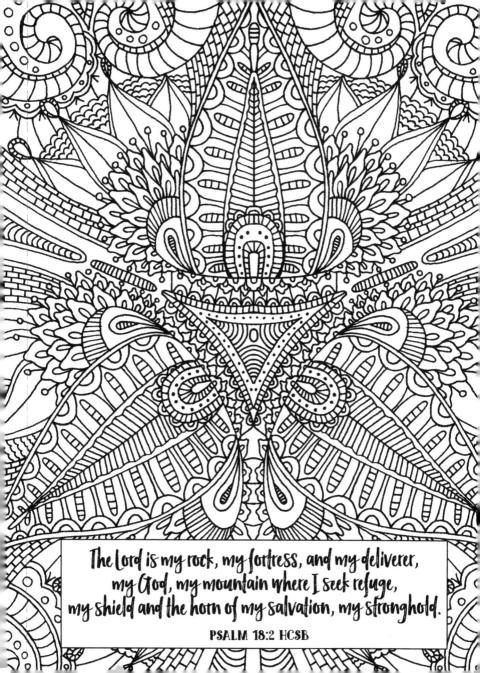

The Lord is my rock, my fortress, and my deliverer, my God, my mountain where I seek refuge, my shield and the horn of my salvation, my stronghold.

PSALM 18:2 HCSB

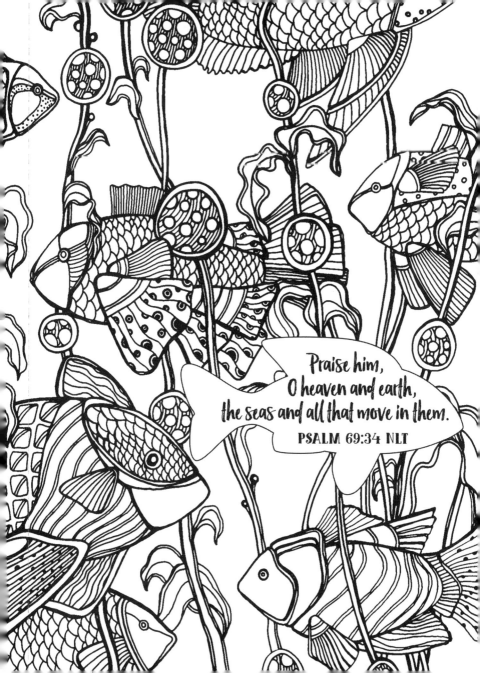

LORD, YOU ARE MY HOPE.
LORD, I HAVE TRUSTED YOU SINCE I WAS YOUNG.

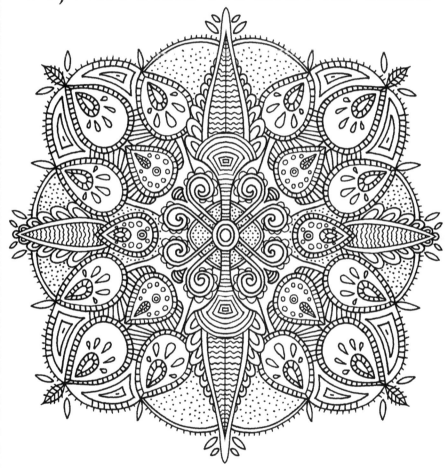

I WILL ALWAYS PRAISE YOU.

PSALM 71:5-6 NCV

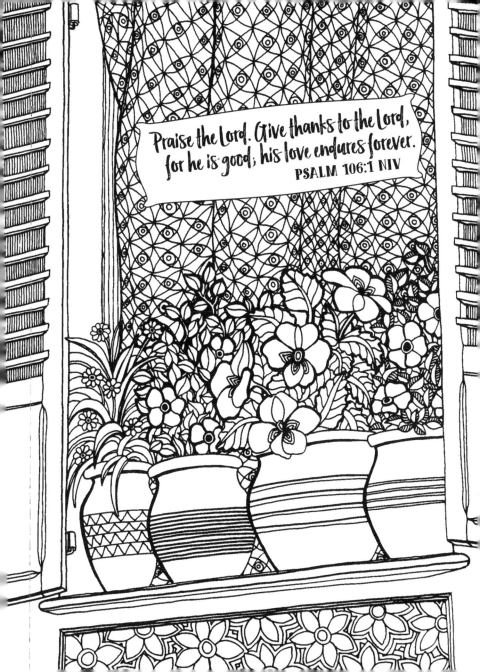

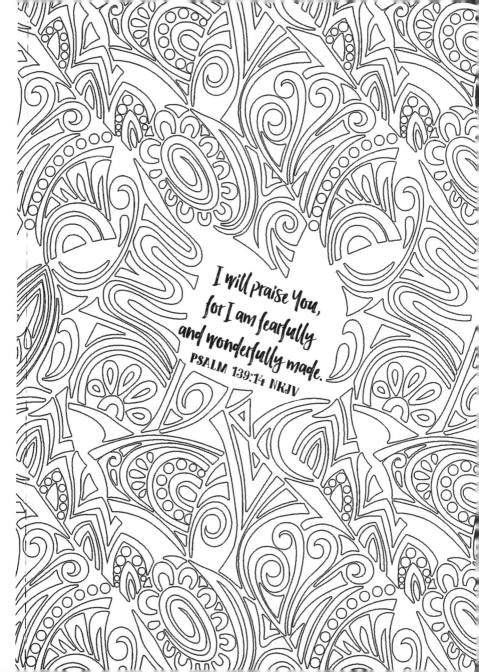

I will praise You,
for I am fearfully
and wonderfully made.
PSALM 139:14 NKJV

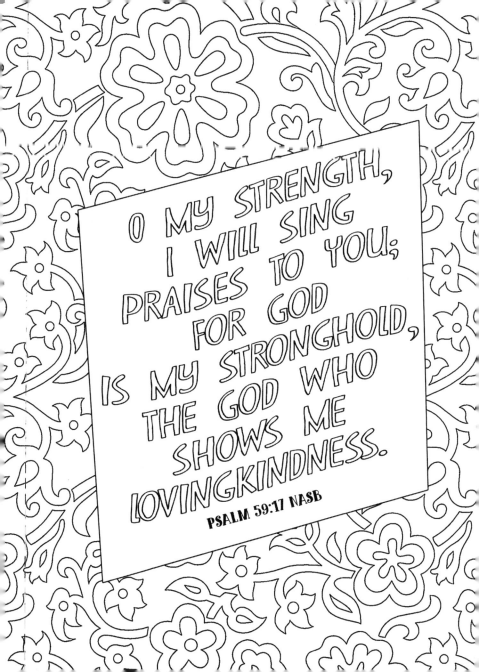

Your kingdom is an everlasting kingdom,
and your dominion endures through all generations.

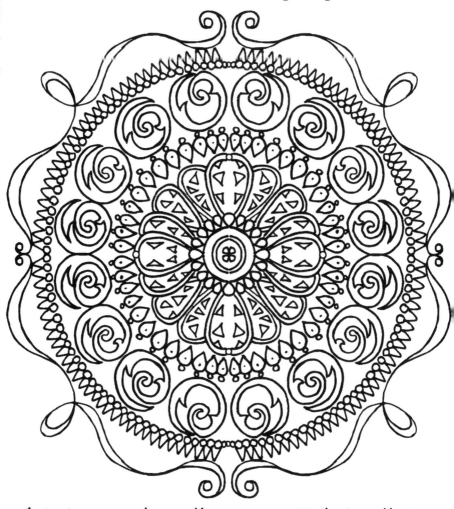

The Lord is trustworthy in all he promises and faithful in all he does.

PSALM 145:13 NIV

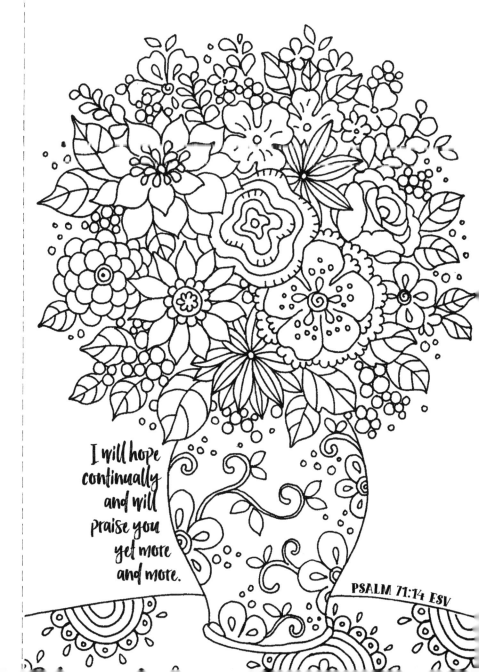

I will hope continually and will praise you yet more and more.

PSALM 71:14 ESV

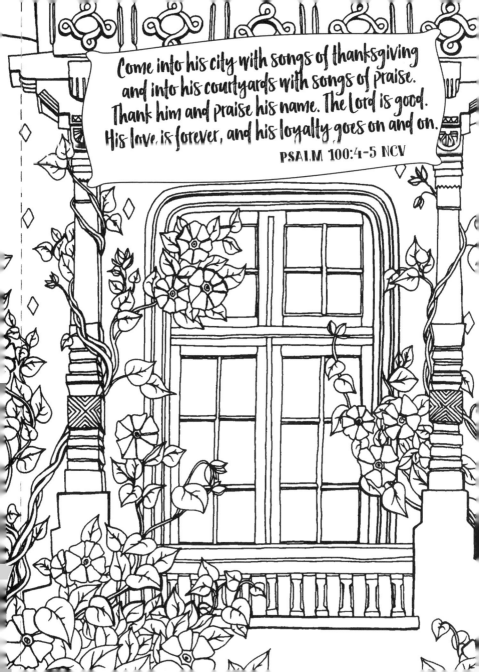

Come into his city with songs of thanksgiving and into his courtyards with songs of praise. Thank him and praise his name. The Lord is good. His love is forever, and his loyalty goes on and on.

PSALM 100:4–5 NCV

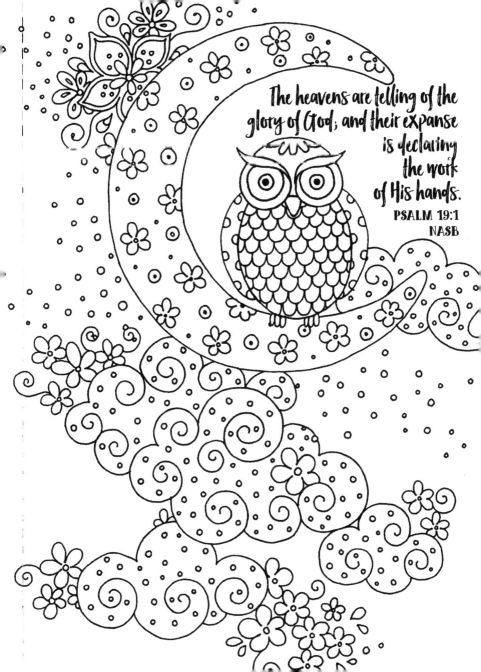

The heavens are telling of the glory of God; and their expanse is declaring the work of His hands.

PSALM 19:1
NASB

I will be filled with joy because of you.

PSALM 9:2 NLT

I will sing praises to your name, O Most High.

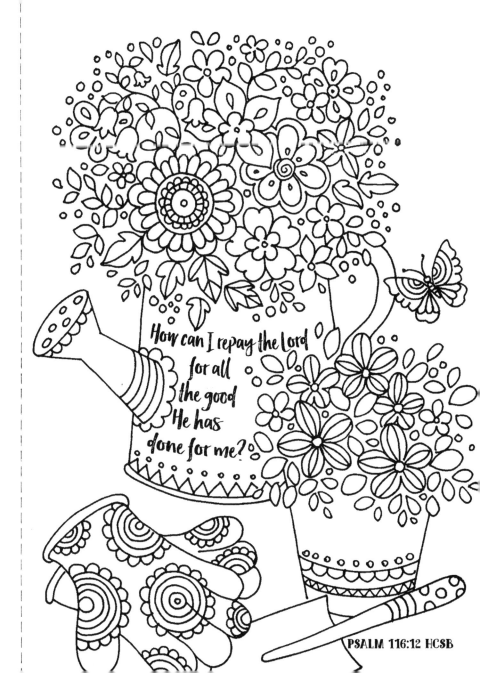

How can I repay the Lord
for all
the good
He has
done for me?

PSALM 116:12 HCSB

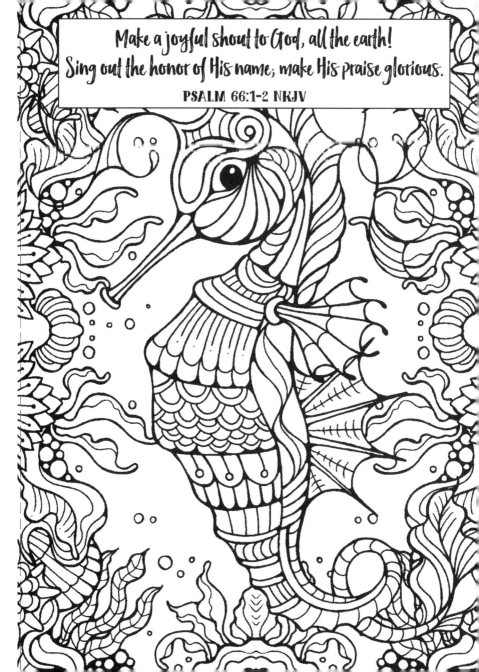

Make a joyful shout to God, all the earth!
Sing out the honor of His name; make His praise glorious.

PSALM 66:1-2 NKJV

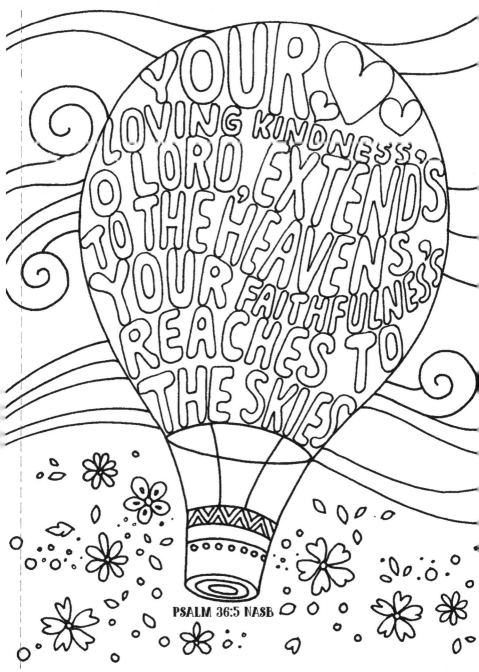

YOUR LOVING KINDNESS TO LORD, EXTENDS TO THE HEAVENS, YOUR FAITHFULNESS REACHES TO THE SKIES

PSALM 36:5 NASB

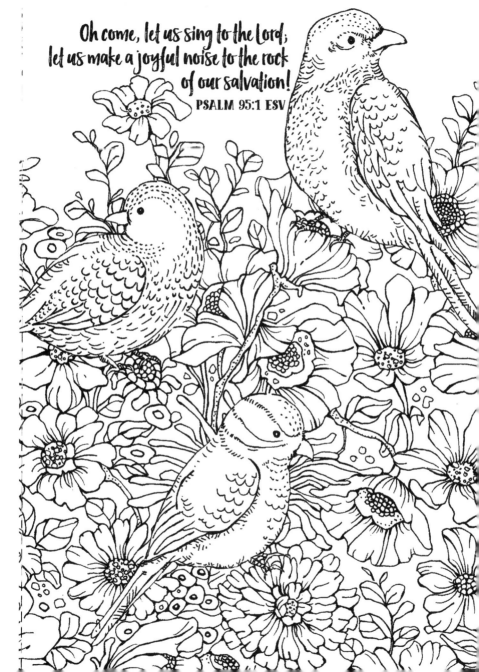

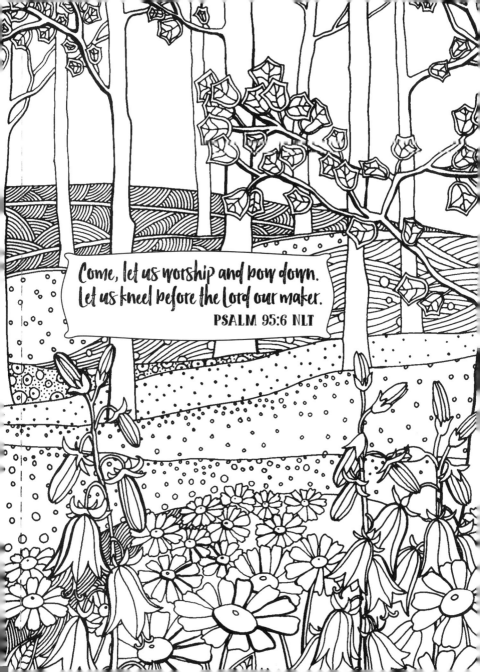

Come, let us worship and bow down.
Let us kneel before the Lord our maker.

PSALM 95:6 NLT

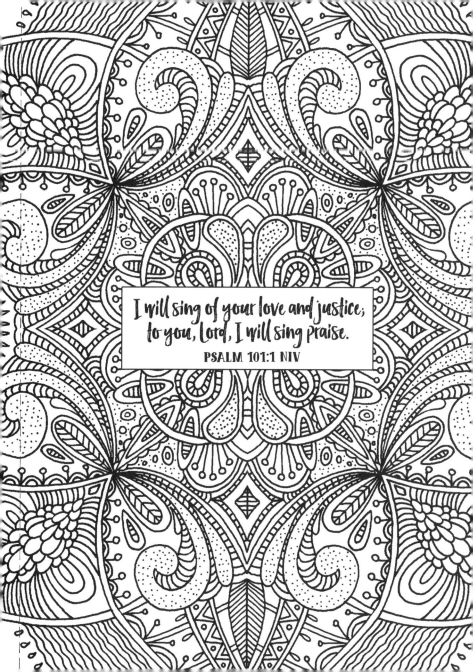

I will sing of your love and justice;
to you, Lord, I will sing praise.

PSALM 101:1 NIV

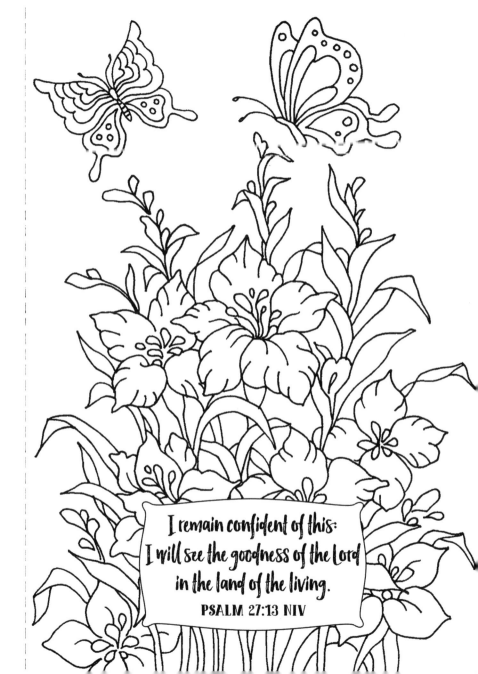

I remain confident of this:
I will see the goodness of the Lord
in the land of the living.

PSALM 27:13 NIV

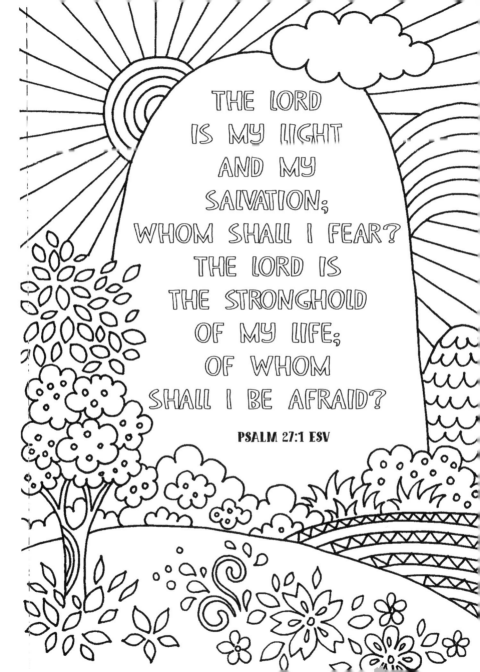

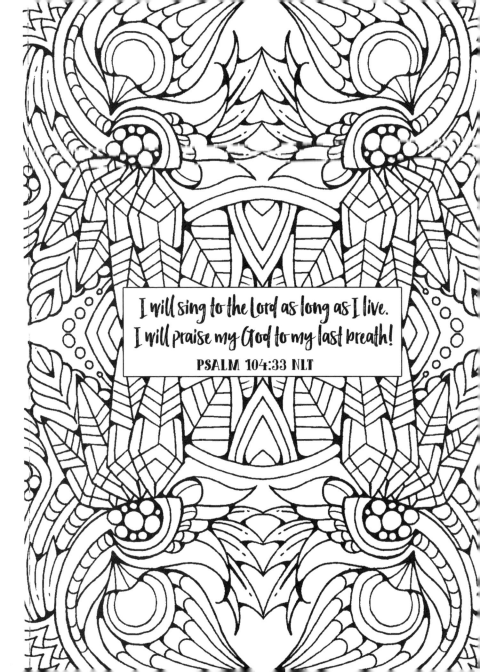

I will sing to the Lord as long as I live.
I will praise my God to my last breath!

PSALM 104:33 NLT

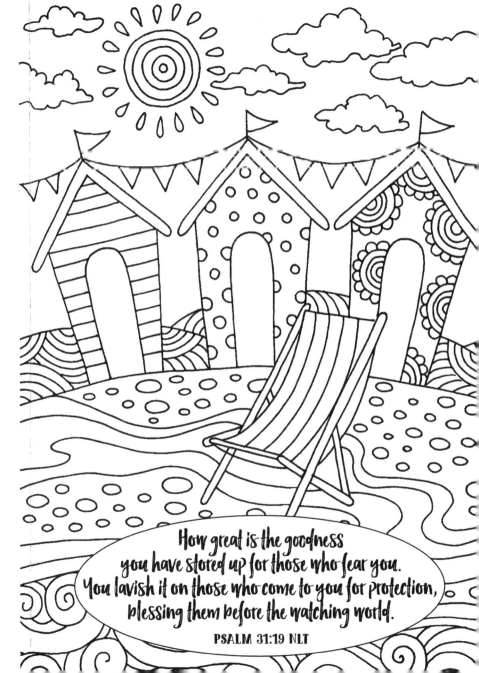

How great is the goodness
you have stored up for those who fear you.
You lavish it on those who come to you for protection,
blessing them before the watching world.

PSALM 31:19 NLT

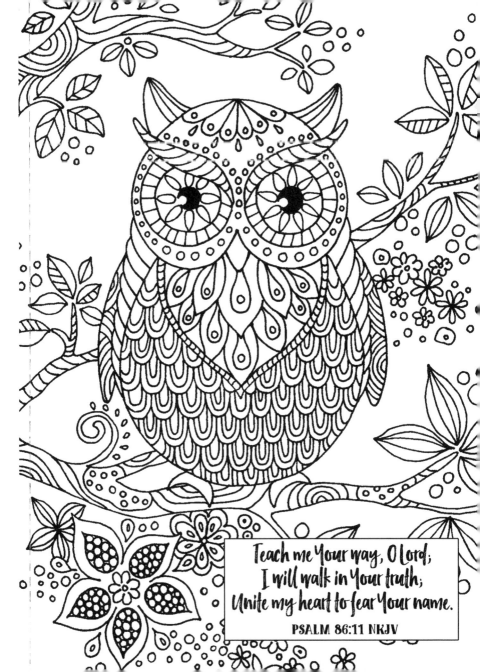

Teach me Your way, O Lord;
I will walk in Your truth;
Unite my heart to fear Your name.

PSALM 86:11 NKJV

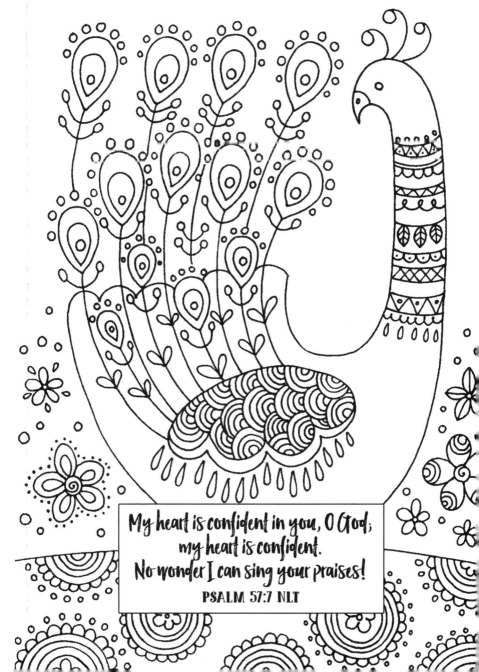

My heart is confident in you, O God;
my heart is confident.
No wonder I can sing your praises!

PSALM 57:7 NLT

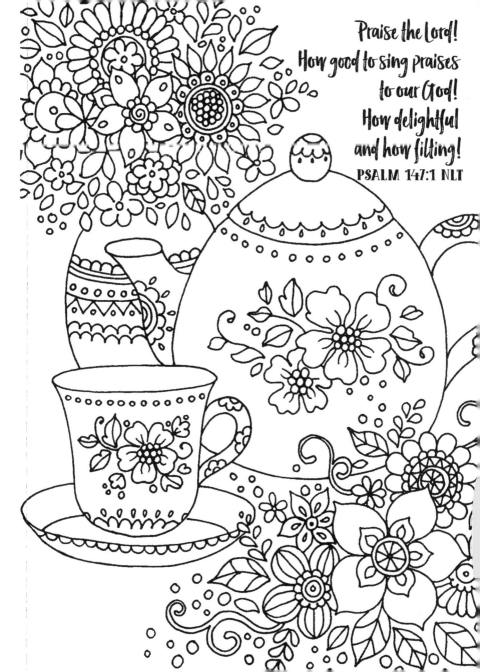

Praise the Lord!
How good to sing praises
to our God!
How delightful
and how fitting!
PSALM 147:1 NLT

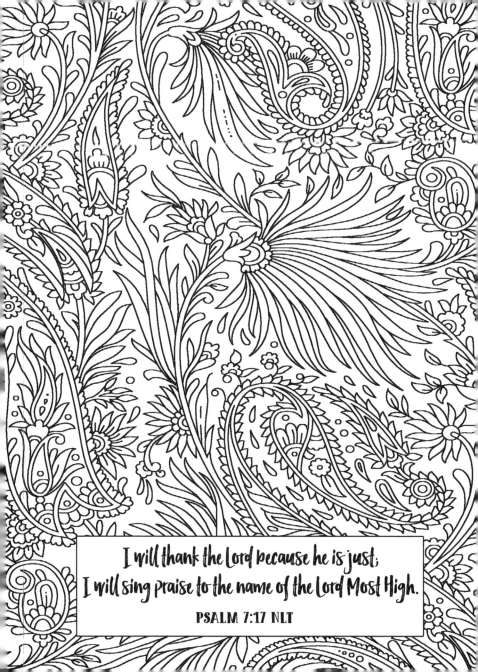

I will thank the Lord because he is just;
I will sing praise to the name of the Lord Most High.

PSALM 7:17 NLT

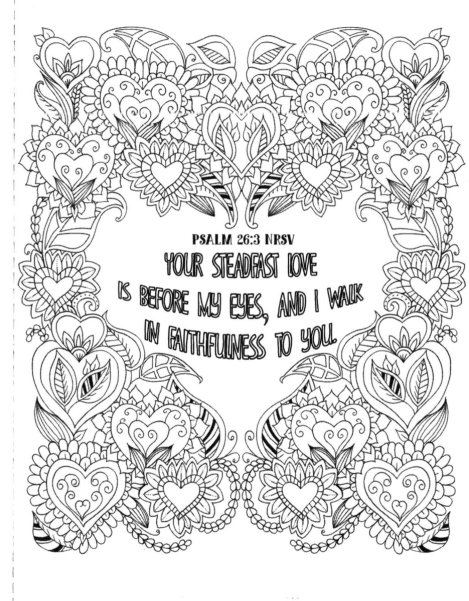

PSALM 26:3 NRSV

YOUR STEADFAST LOVE IS BEFORE MY EYES, AND I WALK IN FAITHFULNESS TO YOU.

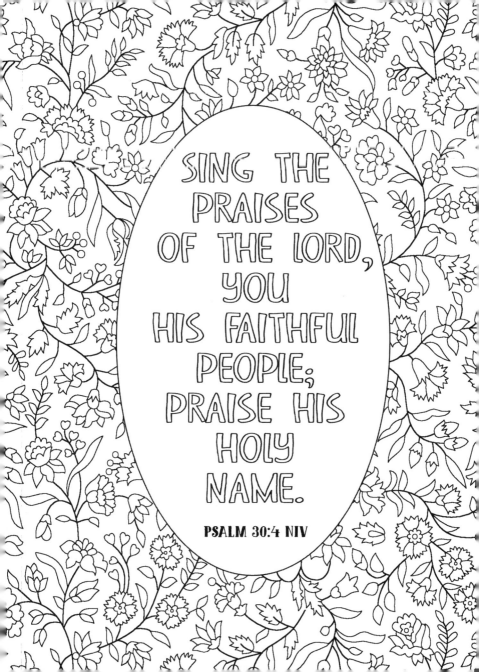

SING THE PRAISES
OF THE LORD,
YOU
HIS FAITHFUL
PEOPLE;
PRAISE HIS
HOLY
NAME.

PSALM 30:4 NIV

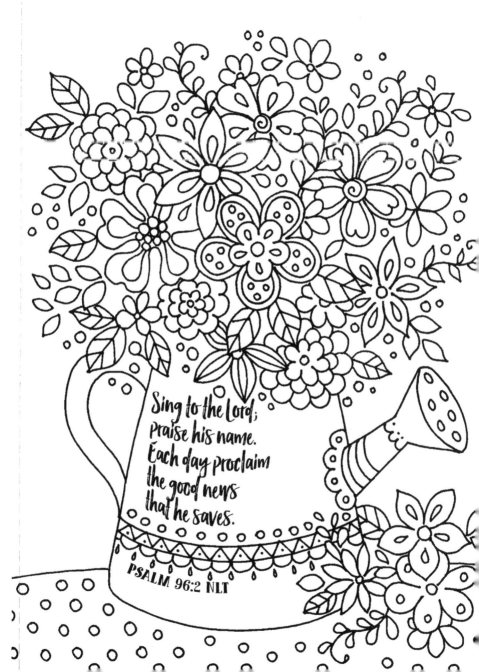

Sing to the Lord;
praise his name.
Each day proclaim
the good news
that he saves.

PSALM 96:2 NLT